When You're Feeling Spiritually Empty

When You're Feeling Spiritually Empty

written by
Craig R. Wagner, O.S.B.

illustrated by
R.W. Alley

ONE
CARING
PLACE
Abbey Press

Text © 2007 by Craig R. Wagner, O.S.B.
Illustrations © 2007 by Saint Meinrad Archabbey
Published by One Caring Place
Abbey Press
St. Meinrad, Indiana 47577

Library of Congress Catalog Number
2007902117

ISBN 978-0-87029-406-8

Printed in the United States of America

Foreword

A healthy spiritual life is essential but not always easy. Boredom, distractions, disappointments, personal sorrows, or simple lack of enthusiasm can threaten to make God seem distant. However, nothing could be further from the truth. God never forgets us, although we often forget God.

The spiritual life is one of mystery, so what may seem like momentary darkness may be calling us to fuller, longer-lasting light. That very emptiness—or hunger—we feel is what invites us to seek God in even deeper ways.

As faith is not about seeing, prayer is not about feeling. You love your family members even when you are not thinking about them—and even when you are angry or disappointed with them! Our relationship with God is similar. We seek a loving union with the God who created us, and we want to live in that love regardless of emotion.

May this book help you see the light through the darkness. And may it provide the assurance that hope indeed surpasses all understanding.

1.

It may be a disappointment in life that has diminished your spirit, or possibly a personal tragedy. It may be that your passion and zest for the spiritual things of life have just mysteriously disappeared. Whatever the reason, know that God hasn't left your side.

2.

You are not abandoned by God! A heart desiring to pray despite spiritual emptiness is one ready to be enlarged by God's love. Let God increase your capacity for love so you may then share it more fully with others.

3.

Even people who devote their entire lives to prayer (monks, for instance) go through "dry" or "empty" periods in their spiritual lives. Many saints became so not because they "felt holy" in prayer but because they achieved holy things through prayer. So, you're in good company.

4.

Your desire to seek God is placed in your heart by God. Occasional frustration with this life is God's way of centering your focus on the life to come. So, you are longing for heaven! Ironically, if you stop seeking peace from the world, you can live peaceably within it, encountering "heaven on earth."

5.

Although dryness in prayer does not necessarily mean that you are at fault, it is possible that some unresolved issue in your life has separated you from experiencing God's presence. Ask God to reveal this to you and show you the way back.

6.

If the "spiritual combat" becomes too much for you, consult a priest or minister. Meeting regularly with a qualified spiritual director can also help you understand the stirrings of your soul. God reaches out to us through such people.

7.

As you struggle with emptiness, perhaps you are fearful that you no longer believe in or love God as you should. Take heart. Your very doubt reveals your love for God, for if you truly didn't love God, you wouldn't be so troubled by it.

8.

It may be hard to understand why God would allow you to feel so alone. Consider this: If the path were always clear and bright, would you ever stop and praise God for making it so? Absence makes the heart grow fonder, as they say.

9.

Perhaps you feel there's no point to praying because you can't see its effects. Your prayer matters, so persist! Recall Scripture's definition of faith: "Faith is the realization of what is hoped for and evidence of things not seen." (Hebrews 11:1)

10.

Don't despair. Every stage of your spiritual journey has purpose. Moving between periods of spiritual "consolation and desolation" is not an unusual experience.

11.

God uses such changes to direct us away from self-reliance toward self-surrender. In fact, saints such as John of the Cross tell us that the "dark night of the soul" is to be preferred over spiritual joy because it is a greater measure of our complete faith in God.

12.

Sometimes we place too much
emphasis on our own efforts.
Relax, be patient, and keep in
mind that prayer is not our
gift to God, but God's gift
to us. Wait and let <u>God</u>
do the work.

13.

God knows and cares about
your struggles. As you
express them, ask God
for enlightenment and
understanding—but above
all, faith, hope, and love.

14.

Sometimes we are simply asked to "be" with God through our spiritual struggles. Center yourself in solitude and trust that, with God's help, you will persevere.

15.

Avoid thinking of prayer only as a way to talk to God. <u>Listening</u> to what God says to our hearts is even more important. Learn to pray in silence so you can hear God's side of the conversation.

16.

Distractions and "the business of the day" can threaten to invade our prayer time. Don't become frustrated. Dismiss such intrusions immediately and center yourself on listening to God alone. With a prayerful heart, you will then be better equipped to "meet the world."

17.

Perhaps your spiritual routine is in a "rut" because it has become too familiar, too "mechanical." Try an alternative approach to gain a different perspective and deeper insight.

18.

Connecting with God can take many forms. Try reading the Psalms on your porch swing; getting on your knees beside your bed for night prayer; imagining yourself in a scene depicted in an inspiring work of art.

19.

Many of us need ritual—meaningful, concrete religious practices and customs—to enliven our faith. Traditional symbols and objects such as candles, icons, and incense can foster a prayerful atmosphere. Sacred music can also help set the tone.

20.

Educate yourself. Many books have been written about prayer, some of the most helpful by saints who themselves experienced spiritual dryness and desolation.

21.

Sometimes we simply need a "jump start." Find a book filled with prayers you haven't heard before, or a book of meditations on the mysteries of God. Let the words soak into your soul in silence, allowing your own prayer to spring up and take root.

22.

Reading Scripture is an excellent way to pray. Slowly read a passage, and reflect on any word or phrase that strikes you. Apply it to your spiritual life. Open your heart to God and allow the words you've read to begin an intimate conversation with your loving Creator!

23.

Since the Bible recounts humanity's struggle in seeking God, you'll see that feeling "spiritually abandoned" is a common experience. Many biblical figures like David and Job experienced God in deeper ways and grew in their faith only after periods of "spiritual exile."

24.

Memories can help you reconnect. Recall your earlier relationship with God, just as you and your spouse might remember the excitement of your days dating one another. The joy you had then is still within you; ask God to help you recapture it and build on it.

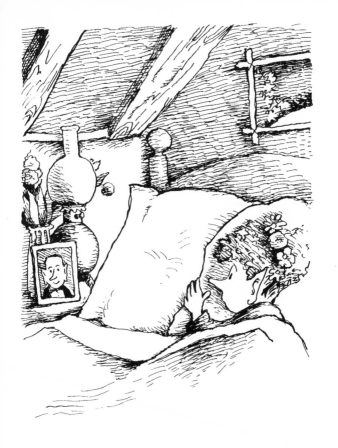

25.

It is common to focus on the negative. Try centering your prayer on thanking God for all the good in your life that comes to mind.

26.

Emerge from your comfort zone to take in the "big picture." Perhaps a walk through the woods or along the lake will regenerate your spirit by reminding you of God's goodness in ways you've taken for granted.

27.

God speaks to us in so many ways. Try using the events and personal encounters of your day as a springboard into prayer. With a little effort, you can become more aware of the ways God works through seemingly ordinary circumstances.

28.

Defining prayer by method, place, or time can be limiting. Consider that your every thought, word, or action is known by God, and make your entire life your prayer. "Use words if necessary," as St. Francis of Assisi said.

29.

Remember that faith is meant to be a shared experience. If praying alone becomes a challenge, connect with others in worship services, Bible study, or prayer groups. Rub shoulders with those who are spiritually alive!

30.

Shift the focus from your own spiritual darkness to being a light for others. A simple act of charity or prayer for someone in need not only connects God to others through you, but can do wonders for your own soul.

31.

Have you ever done something nice for someone although you didn't really feel like it? God delights in such love, and in prayer offered in the same spirit.

32.

By remaining outwardly
joyful and loving despite
interior emptiness, we please
God all the more because it
is the Divine will that
motivates us and not a
sense of our own well-being.

33.

No prayer is more pleasing to God than one offered without expectation of immediate reward. Tell God: "I know you're with me, and that you can hear me even though I feel distant from you. I love you and praise you for your goodness!"

34.

Be confident that God hears you, but make your prayer sincere and concise. Lofty thoughts aren't necessary, only a pure heart. Prayer, St. Benedict said, "ought to be short and pure."

35.

Your struggle to pray makes God proud. Out of love, a mother eventually places the child in her arms on the ground so he or she can learn to walk independently. Likewise, we can only mature spiritually if we learn to pray without assistance. Hidden, God beams at our progress.

36.

God's designs are beyond our limited vision, so we cannot imagine all the good in store for us. Each grain of sand on the beach may not seem like much, but together, they hold back the ocean. Put your trust in God's vision for your spiritual life.

37.

Always remember that God loves you; otherwise, you would not exist! Despite how dry your spirit may be, allow that truth to lift you to new heights!

38.

When spiritual joy returns—
and it will—give thanks to
God! Return your joy in prayer
by asking God to light the way
for others suffering through
spiritual darkness.

Craig R. Wagner, O.S.B., is a former newspaper editor and reporter who experienced a spiritual awakening after the passing of his father in 2003. A native of Findlay, Ohio, he has left behind his 18-year career in journalism and is answering the call to become a Benedictine monk at Saint Meinrad Archabbey, where he is in formation as a novice. Knowing firsthand what it means to experience spiritual dryness as well as joy, he asks that we all pray for one another from God's love for each of us.

Illustrator for the Abbey Press Elf-help Books, **R.W. Alley**, also illustrates and writes children's books, including *Making a Boring Day Better—A Kid's Guide to Battling the Blahs*, a recent Elf-help Book for Kids. See a wide variety of his works at: www.rwalley.com

The Story of the Abbey Press Elves

The engaging figures that populate the Abbey Press "elf-help" line of publications and products first appeared in 1987 on the pages of a small self-help book called *Be-good-to-yourself Therapy*. Shaped by the publishing staff's vision and defined in R.W. Alley's inventive illustrations, they lived out the author's gentle, self-nurturing advice with charm, poignancy, and humor.

Reader response was so enthusiastic that more Elf-help Books were soon under way, a still-growing series that has inspired a line of related gift products.

The especially endearing character featured in the early books—sporting a cap with a mood-changing candle in its peak—has since been joined by a spirited female elf with flowers in her hair.

These two exuberant, sensitive, resourceful, kindhearted, lovable sprites, along with their lively elfin community, reveal what's truly important as they offer messages of joy and wonder, playfulness and co-creation, wholeness and serenity, the miracle of life and the mystery of God's love.

With wisdom and whimsy, these little creatures with long noses demonstrate the elf-help way to a rich and fulfilling life.

Elf-help Books

...adding "a little character" and a lot
of help to self-help reading!

Getting Older, Growing Wiser	#20089
Worry Therapy	#20093
Trust-in-God Therapy	#20119
Elf-help for Overcoming Depression	#20134
New Baby Therapy	#20140
Teacher Therapy	#20145
Stress Therapy	#20153
Making-sense-out-of-suffering Therapy	#20156
Get Well Therapy	#20157
Anger Therapy	#20127
Caregiver Therapy	#20164
Self-esteem Therapy	#20165
Peace Therapy	#20176
Friendship Therapy	#20174
Christmas Therapy (color edition) $5.95	#20175
Happy Birthday Therapy	#20181
Forgiveness Therapy	#20184

Book price is $4.95 unless otherwise noted.
Available at your favorite gift shop or bookstore—
or directly from One Caring Place, Abbey Press
Publications, St. Meinrad, IN 47577.
Or call 1-800-325-2511.
www.carenotes.com